Commissioned to Love

A Collection of Poetry & Prose

by

Carlos Harleaux

COMMISSIONED TO LOVE

Copyright ©2018 by Carlos Harleaux.

Published by 7th Sign Publishing

(www.PeauxeticExpressions.com)

All rights reserved. No part of this book may be reproduced or transmitted in any form or by any means without written permission from the author/and or publisher.

ISBN 978-0-692-96681-5

Book Cover Design and Illustrations by David Boyce.

Photography by Renato Rimach

Introduction

The inception of this book started unlike any other book I have ever written. I was commissioned to write some poems for a specific purpose, but that eventually fell through. I was disappointed at the time about the way things turned out. Then, it hit me. This is something I needed to share on my own. I added more poems to it, in addition to some essential quotes that would serve the primary purpose of uplifting women.

I believe that now, more than ever, women need to be reminded of their strength and worth. Reality TV and social media tell us that women are only good for being a trophy on a man's arm, exploitation and causing drama. That narrative must change.

Men should be commissioned and charged to uplift the women in their lives. Women need it desperately, without prompting. The poems included in this book center around an overall commission to inspire, to dream and most of all, to love.

Dedicated To You

I dedicate this collection of poetry to women everywhere who go beyond the call of duty to be wonderful grandmothers, mothers, wives, girlfriends, sisters, aunts, teachers, professionals and all-around superwomen. Your beauty and efforts do not go unnoticed. This is for you.

Table of Contents

Who Is She?	8
Excuse Me	10
You Earned It	12
Sadly Mistaken	14
Unparalled	17
*The Sign of Completion	19
Butterfly	21
Don't Forget To Look Up	24
Your Worth	26
Every Queen	29
The Definition Of	31
Treat Her As Such	34
I Don't Belong Here	36
She Is Not Extinct	39
*I Just Want You To Like Me	41
Full Bloom	43
Just In Case	46
Giving Love Another Chance	48
Permission	51

*Everybody Plays The Fool	53
Don't Run	55
Break Your Smile	57
Lost	59
Empty	61
Instalove	64
Mirror	65
Water Your Seed	67
Dark Nights	69
Not Your Concern	71
The Affirmation	73
*Your Words Have Power	75

*Denotes original essays

Who Is She?

She is precise with her diction
And calculated with her speech
Her stride is graceful and poised
As she glides across the room
Just like she was walking on air
Her beauty is unmatched
And can't be bought off the rack
Her smile is a radiant beacon of light
Despite the sting of life's daggers
Piercing her back
She actively seeks ways to
Dodge conformity
Because she is an original masterpiece
That can never be duplicated
Only hopelessly imitated
She is worthy on all occasions
To be celebrated
Her head is adorned with a crown
Containing the most precious jewels
This side of heaven has ever witnessed

She is irresistible
Like bees grasping onto the
Slow, warm drip of a honey comb
Who is she, you ask?
She is your exalted, breathtaking queen

Excuse Me

Excuse me, Queen
May I have this dance?
Would you grant me
Just this one chance
To stand amidst your glow
And be overwhelmed
By your beauty and radiant splendor
No other name could
Dare explain your regal reign
Oh, how I envy the fabric
That rests upon your
Gracious feminine curves
I love to get lost in
The depths of your gaze
As your eyes testify for
All you have endured
Without ever having to
Utter a word
Excuse me, Queen
Would you grant me the honor

Of getting just a fraction
Of your time?
You move me
You inspire me
You ignite me
You excite me
I am better for knowing you
You have forever enriched my life

You Earned It

For all the times
You cried solemn tears
Alone in the dark
While everyone else was
Sound asleep
For the way you use
Just two hands to
Perform the work of eight
Bruised, broken and disappointed
Yet and still you refuse to hate
For your brilliant mind
And energetic spunk
Sexy swagger
And the space in your heart
Only expanded
It never shrunk
For being the father
When Daddy wasn't around
For being discriminated against
But choosing to wear a smile

Instead of a frown
Though you may have been
Feeling down
You kept your head held
High and your faith
Kept you walking for miles
Until your feet were sore
And calloused
But no more
There are brighter days ahead
You have more than earned your crown

Sadly Mistaken

You must have me mistaken
For a lesser girl
Step up to the major leagues
And recognize this world class woman
I have no need for your
Tangible possessions
Because truth be told
I could buy you if I really wanted to
Please, whatever you do
Don't allow your mind to
Wander into the deceptive idea
That you can slither and
Slick talk you way
Into my heart
Let alone my bed
If you are privileged enough
To unlock any part of me

Consider yourself blessed
You must earn this seat
Next to me
My love doesn't come free

Bring more to the table than mediocrity.
Be unforgettable.

Unparalled

Please don't insult my existence
By insinuating any form of familiarity
I am uniquely made
Insatiable craved
My respect will not be compromised
Never behind the curtain
Because I am always center stage
The flow of my hair
The fire in my eyes
The voluptuous fullness of my lips
Which speak poignant words
Like warm molasses
Dripping all over your soul
I am unlike anything
You have ever seen, felt or smelled
Can you catch whiff of this greatness?
Inhaling the sweet fragrance
Of royal bliss

You wish you had one as
Breathtaking as this
Know her worth or
Become a casualty of it

The Sign Of Completion

There are countless women in today's society who are at the top of their game. Women have come a long way with the rights and power they now possess. People don't flinch anymore to see a woman as a CEO, highly paid entertainer or even the head of her household. Notice I didn't say breadwinner, but head of the household. That's a totally different story that I won't get into here.

Nevertheless, women are powerful and taking charge like never before. Ironically, there has been a dramatic decline in the sense of self-worth for women. Don't believe me? Just take a look at social media. Successful and gorgeous women are stooping to standards beneath their worth just to say they have a man.

I truly don't understand the sense of desperation many women have today. My only rationale is the fact that women still outnumber men. Maybe some women think there aren't enough men to go around. Who knows? A woman who wants a man (while keeping her composure as the lady that she is to get him) wins over the woman who does whatever she can to get a man she can't live without.

At the end of the day, we all have a desire to be wanted.

Butterfly

I can feel this opposing force
Restricting my wings
Preparing me to make my debut
Into this outside world
And when I break free
They will all marvel in awe
And wonder of my marvelous
Intoxicating beauty
My back will be speckled
With the most vibrant colors
That have yet to be seen
I won't be contained
They will all bear witness
Of how I have traveled
Through the fire, unscathed
Unashamed of my testimony
Because my complicated tapestry
Tells my story more descriptively
Than any audible
Words ever could

You can find me floating in
In the air
Just over your shoulders
Sit up, take notice and
Behold such a glorious creation

There's a difference between visualizing your destiny and blazing a path towards it.

Don't Forget To Look Up

I watch you day in, day out
Even you can't seem to figure out how
You push through the pain
Making it invisible for others
To see the strain
All they know are the
Warm smiles
Vibrant laughs and
Heartfelt hugs
Little do they know
When the lights go down
I am the one cradling your spirits
To give you enough gumption
To tell your mountains
To crumble beneath you
I have counted each of your tears
One by one
As they traveled from your
Cheeks to your chest
I am the one who

Keeps your fears contained
When your journey gets weary
And you are in need of rest
Look up
You are royalty
Don't you know?
Look up
Look around to see
You are sun kissed and
Immensely blessed
Look up
Head up
Let the tips of your crown
Touch the sky

Your Worth

Royalty cannot coexist with peasantry
Intelligence cannot be bed partners
With supreme ignorance
A room filled with love
Has no standing room for hate
We cannot take a bold stand
For the principles we know
To be right and true
While simultaneously sitting
In silence with clasped hands
And bitten tongues
Inner beauty does not compete
Against fleeting, carnal, external factors
That are momentarily
Pleasing to the eye
The inner me cannot be elevated
While concurrently being dragged to
The ground by your lowly standards
I am not cocky
I am confident

I am not brazen
But I am intentionally bold
I know my worth
I know who I am
So respect it
And fall in line accordingly

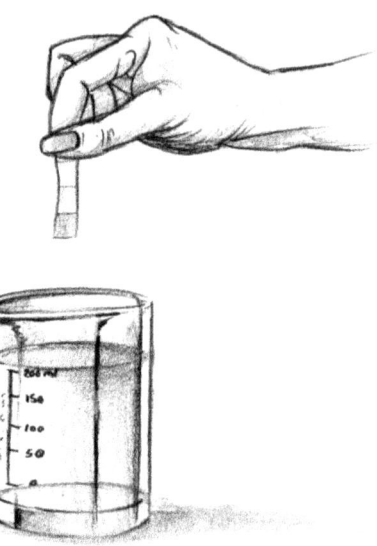

Never let a relationship be the litmus test of your worth.

Every Queen

You know, I am quite capable
Of placing my own crown
Upon my own head
I am able to create my own
Recipes and bake my own bread
I can love free flowingly
Knowingly giving the
Sweetest essence of me
Nurturing my seeds to grow
And become more momentous than I
I can try to do it all with these
Two arms and legs
That operate well beyond their
Natural capability
I am your everyday superwoman
Turning impossible miracles
Into everyday occurrences
At the blink of an eye
I am awe inspiring
For all inquiring

I am authentically that damn good
Honey dipped
Cinnamon dusted
Righteously marvelous to behold
But every queen appreciates
A mighty king to share her throne

The Definition Of...

Her eyes gleam with
Deep, dark, depths of mystery
Her lips, full and supple
Carrying healing elixirs for
Our entire generation to digest
We are birthed from her golden womb
And we stand on the foundation
That securely rests
Upon her shoulders
Her body is a plentiful delight
And oh quite a sight to see
Leaving absolutely not
Another morsel to be desired
Her legs are strong, like stallions
That have served for safe travels
Over troubled waters
Her skin's shimmery tone is
Toasted by the sun
Offering a navigating glow to
Charge us through our course

To greatness
She is bold, but never too proud
She is honest without brutality
She is your mother
Your wife
Your sister
Your aunt
And she knows how to be
All you need as your lover too
She is regal and always poised for greatness
She is all of these things
And we shall call her Queen

Real love will never cause you
to shrink your existence.

Treat Her As Such

You say she is your world
Your lover, your fighter, your ace
Your reason to wake up
Every morning and feel the sun
And subsequently the glow from her aura
Fall freshly on your face
Yet you treat her like peasantry
Excluding all pleasantries
Can't you see she is
Durably delicate
There is only so much
She can take before she breaks
So build her up and
Lift her on high where she belongs
If you make a mistake
By bruising her heart
Stand up, man up
Readily admit your wrongs
It is impossible to lay
Roses, orchids and tulips at her feet

With your words
Yet throw withered and wasteful weeds
In her face
With your actions
That is no way to treat the one
You call exalted
Don't you think?

I Don't Belong Here

When they inquire from the shadows
"Why don't you comply with our rules?"
I smile and remain silent
They call me a prude
I laugh and say
"That may be true"
Before I refute their question
With a more pertinent, burning question
"Why should I try to fit within your moment?"
From my inception
My worth was much more
Than you could hold
With both hands stretched wide
Yet you have the audacity to ask why
I exercise my right
To deny placement within
The cookie cutter puzzle
You have so graciously laid out before me
Oh, wait
Let me guess

That little empty space right there
Is that where I'm supposed to fit in?
I smile, yet again
You still have yet to learn
I am royalty
I am complicated
And audacious, maybe
But there is no other way to be
The moment you realize
Your greatness cannot be contained

Don't apologize for authentic self expression.

She Is Not Extinct

Despite what society
Music video scenes
And inappropriate memes may say
She is not extinct
She stands tall and graceful
Unmistakable to be plucked
From the masses
An anomaly she is
But she is still here
Undoubtedly
Here to guide those
Made in her image
Yes, have somehow lost their way
Along their journey to the land
Of exquisite womanhood
Don't let the skewed statistical data
Make you believe
For one second
That she has vanished
For she is here

Quietly ingesting her surroundings
Calculating with discernment
You may throw sand in her eyes
Or salt on her name
But to count her out
Is a grave mistake
For she is very much alive and well
Changing our world
One day at a time
Just on a grand
And unimaginable scale

I Just Want You To Like Me

Social media has greatly contributed to the decline of women's (and people period) self-esteem in recent years. There is a good side. For instance, people can catch up with long last family and friends, promote their businesses and/or share exciting life moments. However, there is a dark side of influence too.

Many women use various filters and sophisticated photo editing techniques to appear to be someone they are not. Unfortunately, their public lies are plastered all over the internet for mass consumption. The filters and enhancements give an illusion to a life that is not really being lived.

Maybe you're a few sizes up from your glory days. You could be recovering from a nasty divorce or breakup. Or you might be picking yourself back up after being laid off from work. You are still beautiful. You are still strong. You are still worthy.

The best part about it is you are all of these things without any artificial enhancers. Know your worth and don't let social media, anyone or anything define who you are.

Full Bloom

Your petals are outstretched
Towards the sun as if
Mother nature shouted
Hallelujah
Let's all rise to celebrate
This grand occasion
Unbelievably stunning
In every way imaginable
Yet you curl inside
And hide beneath your beautiful
The rain would dance
With just one chance to land
On your sacred skin
A glow so bright
It brings light within
To others who are fortunate enough
To bask in the mere presence
You are quite the gorgeous flower
Yet, why is your head bowed
And your countenance cowered?

Look up
Where your radiance lies
Look up
Now we see those soul piercing eyes
Look up
The sky is waiting to greet you
Look up
The woman inside that
You were destined to be
Would sure like to meet you

Your fiercest competition is the person staring back at you in the mirror, not somebody else.

Just In Case

As the world keeps turning
You keep effortlessly juggling
Business, lover, family, friend
All with a graceful smile
Never a discouraging utterance
Wondering will your hectic race end
Your face shows no traces
Of the many tears you have cried
In the dark
The daggers they threw at your heart
Like a dart
You remained untouched
Pure and unfiltered
And remarkably breathtaking
So in case no one has told you already
You are appreciated
You are desired
You are sexy
You are beautiful
You are amazing

You are lovely
You are hope
You are triumph
You are love

Giving Love Another Chance

I look in your eyes and see
The soul of a woman
Who has endured more than
Her fair share of love scars
You vowed you would never
Give someone else the key to
Your heart again
Or fall into these waters for a fresh start
You didn't have to let your walls down
But you allowed me to
Help you lower them one day at a time
Brick by brick
Inch by inch
You won't have to worry about
Tears in the shadows again
You won't have to question loyalty
Because I'll always be right by your side
Through your pain I still see
A woman who welcomes love
How do you do it?

How do you endure it?
I don't take the privilege
Of holding your heart in my hands lightly
I'll guard it better
Than they ever did
I won't bruise it so carelessly
Like they did
I want to thank you for giving love another chance
Through me

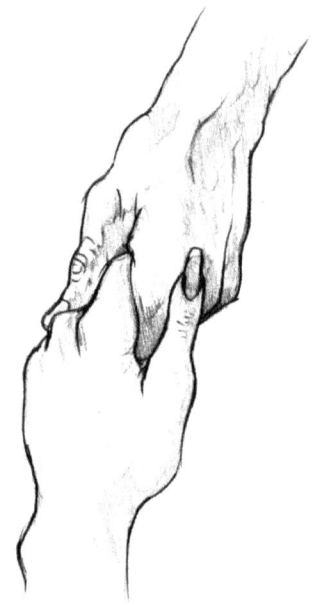

No one can walk through life without lending a chance to trust.

Permission

I grant you the permission to hurt me
Even though I trust that you will not
My precious heart is not a stranger
Of being introduced to its share
Of bruises and battle scars
Yet, I am strong and resilient
The words may burn
The cuts may sting
But I'm looking to you to
Entrap me with your love
Light my soul on fire
With just a silent gaze
Deep into my eyes
I don't let just anybody
Get past the velvet ropes
Surrounding my heart
There's something about you
That makes me believe
I can trust you to be the
Keeper of the keys to my pain

I am trusting you
Something that in the past
Has been more than an ocean to do
But I am trusting you
Will do the right thing

Everybody Plays The Fool

There is a perceived weakness with opening your heart to love. People think that if you give someone a second chance or allow yourself to be hurt, that means you're weak. Some of the strongest people are those that give themselves permission to be hurt. That takes a special courage that frankly many people do not possess.

When it comes to love, it's easy as an outsider to say what you will or won't do. It's easy to say what you will or will not put up with. The truth is everyone plays the fool in the name of love at some point in their life. I like to think of love as everyone being crazy. Yep, that's right. Everyone has some kind of crazy that makes them unique. The trick is being able to find out what kind of crazy you're willing to deal with.

Don't let anyone make you feel less of a person for giving love another chance. As long as the other person is not abusing you, it's frankly no one else's business but yours. Live your life with open hands and no regrets. That's where you will find true fulfillment.

Don't Run

Since when were you created to chase?
Who misinformed you to believe
That you must lower your standards
And accept whatever may come your way?
Who gave you permission to think
Less of yourself than you deserve?
And place yourself beneath your worth?
Priceless
Despite your regal attire
You behave as if you are in dire need
Don't you remember you are
The precious supply
For them to demand
The cream of the crop
If you walk with the grace
Intended for your very existence
The aura of your royalty will glow
And your crown will never drop

Let your presence precede you before entering a room.

Break Your Smile

When your lips part to
Reveal that marvelous glow
It's like hot tea meant to
Soothe the soul
Don't you know who you are
Do you remember whose you are?
It is not the absence of your
Battle scars that help us
Muster up the extra strength to fight
But rather your inviting warmth
That urges us
Charges us forward
And silently speaks that we must
Trudge onward
They may try to chip and
Chisel away your existence
With persistence
But their efforts could never
Take away your brilliance
Remember this if nothing else

To be true
Never let anyone rob you
Of your smile
Even if it's me
And even if it's you

Lost

Can you help me find her?
Just yesterday
I saw her picture again
On the back of a milk carton
Even on such a dulled canvas
Her beauty can still be witnessed
There were no eye witnesses present
To vouch for her disappearance
Let alone her existence
There has been much speculation
Without any concrete confirmation
Some say her soul has sunken inward
This lunging for her has given me
Heart palpitations
I stand here
Drenched in her faded memories
And I raise the question
Have you seen her?
A woman who was once
A radiating masterpiece

Within reflecting outward
Woman who the flowers
Bowed in her presence, wet
With morning dew
If you saw her
You would think the same too

Empty

You poured
You gave repeatedly
You questioned
You waded
In murky waters that you knew
Were beneath your standards
But you were so in love
So into him
So down for the cause
You put on quite a show
Yet no one is left standing
For applause
So you keep praying
Wishing
Hoping
One day he will see
Your efforts and make you
His queen, yet you
Still bow to him who is
Not a king

But much less than a prince
Begging for scraps falling
From his table
Damn
Aren't you tired?
Damn
Aren't you left feeling so uninspired?
Just sifting the remnants of yourself
Into a leaking mold
That could care less to hold your soul
Who gave you permission
To live such an empty existence?

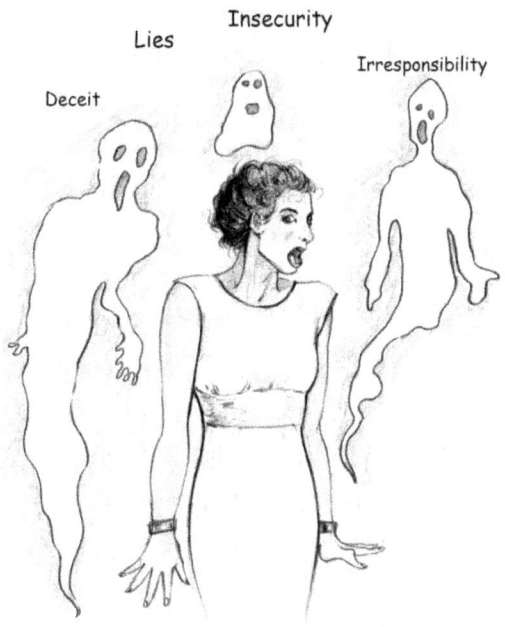

Be careful who you mix soul ties with.
Some are not easily detachable.

Instalove

The clicks and comments
Proclaiming you're a hot thing
Barely 21, your sense of self
Already shot to hell and back
Your reflection even alarming to you
The reason why you don't
Stare directly into the mirror
Afraid to see the true essence
Of the soul housed
Within this carefully crafted shell
Ghosts in the machine
Look beneath the MAC to see
What lies beneath that smile
And what you're worth really means
Push up bras still won't lift
Your self-esteem up where it belongs
Focusing on the artificial
Never knowing that
The problem was skin deep all along

Mirror

Looking in the mirror
And all you see are flaws
Comparing yourself
To snapchat filtered beauty queens
Who don't have a thing to offer
But their body
And you let it crush your
Spirit and mind
Everything on you is placed perfectly
Where it's supposed to be
Without any alteration needed
Celebrate your inner beauty
And the radiance of your exterior
Just the sight of you makes
Men weak in the knees
But you're too tangled in
Your own self-inflicted web of deceit
You can't see
Make them love you exactly for
Who you are

Without any artificial sweeteners
And enhancements
That are at best subpar
Don't stand in the way
Of your own self worth

Water Your Seed

You spend so much precious time
Meeting the needs, wants
And expectations around you
And you've grown accustomed
To the rigorous hustle and bustle
Of serving the needs of others
Always remembering to water
Their doubts so they won't fester
And let the sun in to gently
Burn away their fears
Yet you are hurting
Who tends to the gardener?
Who nurtures the one
Who picks the weeds?
Tills the seeds
And prunes the leaves
Someone must water
The waterer
It's way past due for you
To take care of yourself too

There's a difference between visualizing your destiny and blazing a path towards it.

Dark Nights

It may seem dark
And you may have felt
You've lost your way
Wandering in the wilderness
Wondering when you'll ever
See the light of day
Though you can't see it
Your breakthrough
Is in your pull through moment
On the other side
Silence the voices
Full of doubt
That fill your head
Hold your faith up high
You're getting closer with each step
Blazing your unique path
To your own destiny
One day they will ask you

How you did it
They will question how
You made it through
You are stronger than you know

Not Your Concern

Don't concern yourself
With the grace in which she stands
Your throne is unique
And was created especially for you
Her regal robe was not meant
To adorn your shoulders
You were torn from a different cloth
Beautiful, delicate and breathtaking
In your own light
Don't envy her shoes
Because you know not the
Length of miles
She has walked in them
The price of what you view
As her glorious reign
May be more than you are
Willing to endure to attain

There's no need to covet her crown
Unless you're willing to make
The same sacrifices she made
To wear it

The Affirmation

I am beautiful
I am worthy to be loved
I am unapologetic about
Living my life on the terms
That are best for my destiny
I am comfortable in my own
Glorious skin
Loving every perfect imperfection
Of the existence of my being
I am more than enough
I will not settle for
Less than I deserve
I am empowered to live
In the passion that burns like
A fiery furnace within me
I am a wealth of intelligence
And sexual decadence
I am rich and creamy
Like milk and honey

So don't water me down
Within me I have found
A woman overflowing with purpose
And perpetual fortitude

Your Words Have Power

The most successful people in the world have some common threads. One of the most important things they possess is the power of the tongue. They speak their success into existence. There is a power in the words we speak that we must recognize. I often have to catch myself and fix my words to avoid putting something negative out into the atmosphere.

Yes, God has all control. However, I think we can all agree that we don't want to speak any unnecessary harm that may come our way. This is why I believe affirmations are so important. We often times have to reprogram our minds to think positively against the negativity others may have told us or even worse, what we have placed against ourselves.

If you want it, speak it! It's just that simple. Make your desires known and a reality. Be careful of the words you speak because today, because they shape your tomorrow. Pick a few positive affirmations, repeat them daily, and see watch where your life takes you!

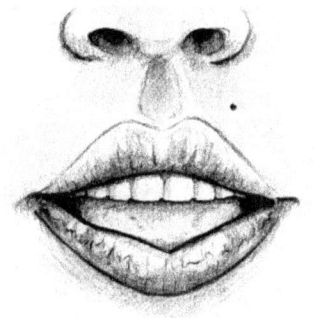

Speak the life you want into existence.
It works!

Here's a sneak peak into the last installment of the *Fortune Cookie* novel series. Look for *When The Cookie Crumbles* soon!

****

"Cookie. Cookie. It's just me. It's me, Sheila. You're going to be ok. Don't move too fast. You're going to throw off your equilibrium again," Sheila said, wiping tears from her eyes.

Bill was holding Cookie's hand tightly. Sean was trying his best to entertain Breanna. His heart really went out to her, as he was sure this had to be a very confusing time for such a young child. Cookie looked over and smiled at Breanna, trying to stop her tears. Finally, she couldn't hold back any longer.

"Ken? I need Ken. Somebody please go find him for me. I can't make it without him. Who's going to help me with Breanna? Ken, please baby come back," Cookie pleaded, with burning tears streaming from her eyes to her ears.

Bill, Sheila and Sean all looked at each other with an awkward silence. No one really knew what to say to keep Cookie calm. Yet again, she suffered another blow to her ever-complicated life. They weren't sure she would bounce back from this one intact though.

"Baby, Ken is gone now. He's watching over you and Breanna. He's watching over all of us. I can just hear him now trying to get me to sit down when he thought I was doing too much. We are all going to miss him. I'm going to miss my son dearly," Bill replied, with a cracked voice. The fact that Bill even showed so much emotion towards Ken's passing proved that he really did love him like his own child. He was the only man that gained his approval for Cookie, even when his own dark secret was revealed.

His insides were turning flips as he watched his daughter cry out helplessly, while his granddaughter looked on in disbelief. Cookie continued to lay on the hospital bed, sobbing uncontrollably. If only there were something she could have done to save him. She would likely always feel like her efforts were not enough. Cookie had to live with the fact that she was the one that pushed Ken over the edge, never to return again.

About The Author

Carlos Harleaux is a native of Houston, TX, now residing in Dallas, TX. He is the CEO of 7th Sign Publishing. *Commissioned to Love* is his seventh release. Carlos's previous works include *No Cream In The Middle*, *Stingrays*, *Fortune Cookie*, *Honesty Box*, *Hindsight 20/20* and *Blurred Vision*. His next book, *When The Cookie Crumbles*, is coming soon. Find out more about Carlos at his website, www.peauxeticexpressions.com.

www.ingramcontent.com/pod-product-compliance
Lightning Source LLC
Chambersburg PA
CBHW072104290426
44110CB00014B/1820